CREDIBLE
RESEARCH
MADE EASY

CREDIBLE RESEARCH
MADE EASY

A Step by Step Path to Formulating Testable Hypotheses

DORCAS MLADENKA

iUniverse, Inc.
Bloomington

Credible Research Made Easy
A Step by Step Path to Formulating Testable Hypotheses

iUniverse books may be ordered through booksellers or by contacting:

iUniverse
1663 Liberty Drive
Bloomington, IN 47403
www.iuniverse.com
1-800-Authors (1-800-288-4677)

ISBN: 978-1-4759-2030-7 (sc)
ISBN: 978-1-4759-2031-4 (ebk)

Printed in the United States of America

iUniverse rev. date: 04/28/2012

CONTENTS

ACKNOWLEDGEMENTS

Here's to my many students who have toiled through the course during my classroom career. Thanks for helping me keep my presentations (both written and spoken) clear and on task. I hope that your journey has taken you to a good place.

I owe a deep gratitude to Leslie (f.t.) and Marilyn. I hated you both for cutting me loose, but I guess it was time to get back on my own journey.

Thanks to Wikipedia and Stat Trek for the distribution images.

Finally, I could not have completed this new version without the strong and unfailing encouragement of my friend Chris.

INTRODUCTION

This workbook is designed to aid you in developing a total research project: from having in mind a specific subject to research (this is your *dependent variable—DV*) to the various influencing factors (your *independent variables--IV*) to determining the relationships among them. Your research will be credible to the extent that you determine *significance* of the influencing factors.

The workbook will take you through the steps of designing and completing a research project. This workbook illustrates, by way of a sample "pretend" research project, a step-by-step progression in determining the variables that may be influencing a specific subject of research, the gathering of data, and what it means to test the "significance" of that influence. To complete your own project you can use this sample to guide you through the steps. If you have a personal or work-related project in mind, you can copy the steps of the sample project in your own project as you go along—whatever feels comfortable to you. But don't skip any steps—they will catch up with you in the end and give you much confusion and grief.

Some research is "descriptive" in nature: you gather and report the data. *Your* research is "analytical" in nature: you will analyze the relationships among variables. You will do this through hypothesis testing.

The Appendix includes an outline and example of this type of research *report*. You can refer to it and see that the format follows the steps outlined here.

The following sections are arranged here in the same sequence you will follow in completing your research project.

> <u>A Sample Project</u>
> ⇨ <u>Research Design</u>
> ⇨ <u>Research Questions</u>
> ⇨ <u>Measurement of Variables</u>
> ⇨ <u>Operational Definitions</u>

Formulating the Hypotheses

⇨Types of Statistical Tests
⇨ Formulating and Stating the Hypotheses

⇨ Collecting the Data: Questionnaire
⇨ Data Preparation and Tally
Overview: Theoretical Distributions
Notes on Data Analysis and Testing for Significance

I strongly suggest that you follow the steps of the "pretend" sample all the way through. Set for yourself a goal not to proceed until you have finished each step. Stop and think about what's going on . . . why a step is important . . . how it fits into the research process. You might want to develop your own project as you go along from step to step, but stay with the sample as well. Your research will go better for you if you proceed in an **orderly fashion**.

A Note: Prof. M's sample research project may seem, well, a bit elementary. This is by design. The variables are chosen in such a way that they will require the most commonly-used statistical tests (which are listed in the workbook).

A real research project on your part will probably be more complicated; however, you will use the same types of variable measurements and the theory will apply in the same way. The "sample" in Prof. M's research was kept uncharacteristically small so as not to clutter the points being made (probably—and certainly—why no results were significant—more on that later.)

You should *google* some information, not included here, about sample size for credible research. Samples don't have to be huge, but they do have to be *representative* of the population: no bias of any kind! **A good sample means everyone in your population had an equal chance of being in the sample**.

PART 1

A SAMPLE PROJECT;
DEFINING AND MEASURING VARIABLES

Professor M teaches the business research course. She wants all of her students to do well in the course, and she wonders what elements might account for differences in their success levels. The problem area, then, is the research course and the success (or failure) of students taking the course.

Professor M decides that "success" in the course (DEPENDENT VARIABLE—DV) would have to be determined by the final grade in the course. She also decides, upon reflection, that since all students get the same material and the same assistance in the course, there may be other elements (INDEPENDENT VARIABLES—IVs) involved. She determines to explore these variables through an analytical, investigative research project.

You will use Professor M's research project as a sample to follow in doing your own research. This first section will include the following:

   ⇨ **Research Design**
   ⇨ **Research Questions**
   ⇨ **Measurement of Variables**
   ⇨ **Operational Definitions**

THE RESEARCH DESIGN

Let's assume the following research design. Prof. M is interested in what variables influence the grade that research students made in the business research course (your *dependent variable).* She selects five *independent variables* to include in her research, and a diagram of her research model looks like this.

Gender

Major

Semester Hrs   Research Grade

Study for the Course

Interest in Statistics

(IVs)   (DV)

PROBLEM STATEMENT: (Ask a question about the variables) To what extent do the variables of gender, major, course load, study, and interest in statistics predict the final research grade.

THE RESEARCH QUESTIONS
(Another way of explaining your research Design)

You will now make the sample project *your* research as you study the process. You are theorizing relationships among your variables.

You are interested in the relationship that each of the IVs had to the dependent variable: how does each IV relate to the research grade? You will indicate the kind of relationship you are interested in researching by formulating questions—the research questions. In order to do that you will of course need a measurement of each variable, and that measurement has to be a *quantity—a number.*

RQ 1 So lets get started, first of all, what do you mean by the variable. When you say "research grade," you mean, of course, the average (mean) research grade made by students . . . and you must specify, for example, students who took the course in the last two semesters: Spring XX or Fall XX.

Your first research question of interest then is a research grade—a very quantifiable measure. The mean of all the research grades in your sample is the measure for your DV.
(The next section is on Measurement Scales and Operational Definitions)

RQ 2 Was there a difference between male and female research grades? (IV Gender: DV Grade)

RQ 3 Did the research grade differ according to the students' majors? (IV Major: DV Grade)

RQ 4 Did the total number of semester hours a student carried during the semester the research was taken influence the research grade? (IV Semester Hrs.: DV Grade)

RQ 5 Did the amount of Study have an influence on the research grade?
First you have to "clean up" ambiguous terms: amount . . . study . . .
By "amount" do your mean how many hours or how often?
By "study" do you mean specifically studying research?
(IV Study: DV Grade)

RQ 6 Was there an association between how "interested in statistics" the student was and that student's research grade?
Again you have to make clear what "interest" really means.
(IV Interest in Statistics: DV Research grade.)

Good news: you are getting closer to developing hypotheses for your research project.

So far you have formulated six research questions: one having to do with data for the DV, the other five having to do with the relationship of each IV to the DV. In order to learn how to do a few more statistical tests, you will also look at relationships of one IV to another IV. There is, however, a more important reason for doing this. You will have collected the data, so it will be a simple matter to do the relationships. And you might find some surprises.

In this example we will add the following research questions:

RQ 7. Were marketing majors "more interested" in learning research than other majors? (IV 2: IV 5)

RQ 8 Was there a difference in study times between male and female students? (IV 1 : IV 4)

There are two things you must do before your begin stating your research questions in the form of hypotheses.
1. You must be very precise about what you mean by the variable because you have to quantify it--make it measurable--one number for each variable.
2. You must determine how you will "tap" the variable—how you will collect the data.

The next two sections will help you perform these two tasks.

MEASUREMENT SCALES

Once you have determined the variables to use in your study, the big challenge is to "tap" them—to get the data on them. The data you get has to be in quantitative form—in numbers to feed into the computer.

NOTE: You won't be having to use formulas to work the tests—computers do that for you. A common software for this type of research is SPSS—available in schools and businesses. There are several measurement scales that are used in research. The most common are

> **nominal**: the variable has no quantitative value as such;
> the variable is divided into groups, such as
> gender MALE / FEMALE
> (*divides sample into categories*)

> **ordinal**: no quantitative value; ranks preferences

> Rank the following cereals in order of your personal preference
> ____cheerios
> ____bran flakes
> ____corn flakes

> (*differences; median*)

> **interval**: no quantitative value, number scale to show importance:

How much do you agree with the company's health insurance plan?

Strongly disagree	Disagree	Neutral	Agree	Strongly Agree
1	2	3	4	5

> (*can yield a mean on the scale*)

> **ratio**: meaningful measurement scale--absolute zero point

> (*research grade: ____*)

> (*can yield a mean*)

It is important to use the measurement scale that will give you the information you seek. Thus every variable has to be "operationally" defined.

DORCAS MLADENKA

OPERATIONAL DEFINITIONS

Every variable has to be operationally defined: for you so that you know what type of test to use . . . and for the reader of your research. The reader of your research has to know precisely what you mean by the variable.

There are numerous types of statistical tests available to the researcher. In this workbook sample you will use a selected few. The tests you will use are commonly-used tests and cover a variety of possibilities for the way you might design your study. Learning how to use a few tests will also make it easier to learn additional tests as you need them.

> The type of statistical test you use depends on the measurement scales that you used to tap your variables.

In order to know what statistical test to use and how to formulate your hypotheses, it is important to remember how you can tabulate and summarize using the various measurement scales.

NOMINAL: categories; groups; "samples"
            (categories cannot be averaged)

INTERVAL and RATIO: numbers
            (you can get a mean)

The way each variable was measured will dictate the *type of relationship* you will establish.

When you relate one variable to another, you look at how both variables were measured and that determines what kind of relationship you can make.

```
V1 ---------- > V2
 \             \
 \             \
 scale?        scale?
```

For example, you measured our DV, GRADES, using the ratio scale. You measured GENDER nominally. How do we relate GENDER to GRADES?

GENDER	RESEARCH GRADER
(nominal)	**(ratio)**

GENDER broke our sample into two groups. We can look at the "mean grade" for males and the "mean grade" for females and see the difference. The software will simply list all the male grades and get a mean, list all the female grades and get a mean, and show you the difference.

Each nominal variable breaks your sample into two or more populations. When related to a ratio or interval scale, the relationship is a **DIFFERENCE OF MEANS**

Sometimes both variables are measured using a nominal scale: GENDER and STUDY.

GENDER	STUDY
(nominal)	**(nominal)**

Since you cannot get a "mean" from categories, you cannot apply a "means test," but you can use a test that will count the frequencies of the categories and determine whether the variables had anything to do with each other. **This relationship is a TEST OF "INDEPENDENCE."**

SEMESTER HOURS and GRADES are both measured with a ratio scale. Neither measurement breaks the samples into groups. Instead, each gives us the "mean" for the whole sample.

SEM HRS	GRADES
(ratio)	**(ratio)**

The type of relationship to establish here is to see if there is a **correlation**--to see whether the two variable *means* move up at the same rate, or down at the same rate, or whether as one moves up the other moves down.

INTEREST is measured using the interval scale, which also yields a mean. So INTEREST and GRADES would also be tested for **correlation**.

INTEREST

GRADES

(interval)

(ratio)

The type of relationship established in both of the above pairs of variables is a **TEST OF CORRELATION**.

IMPORTANT: Each test is suited for a specific type of comparison. The variable measurements determine:

THE MEAN OF A POPULATION
THE INDEPENDENCE OF TWO VARIABLES
THE CORRELATION OF TWO VARIABLES
A DIFFERENCE OF MEANS OF TWO POPULATIONS

TWO VARIABLE TESTS (BIVARIATE TESTS) compare the *means* of *two or more populations*

TESTING DIFFERENCES

Two Sample T Test compares the difference between the means
of *two populations*

ANOVA compares the differences between the means
of two or more populations

TESTING INDEPENDENCE

Chi Square tests for whether variables measured in nominal
scale have an impact on one another

**Two Sample
T Test** compares the difference between the means
of *two populations*

TESTING CORRELATION

**Pearson's r
Correlation** tests whether two variables are correlated

ONE VARIABLE TEST (UNIVARIATE TESTS)

**One Sample
T Test** predicts a mean

Research question No. 1 asked about the mean RESEARCH GRADE; in other words, your hypothesis will make a prediction about the variable. Only one variable is involved, so that requires a "one variable test" (above). All the other predictions will involve two variables and require "two variable tests" (above).

The table below gives a quick look at what test to use depending on how the variables are measured.

<table>
<tr><td colspan="2" align="center">**SHORTHAND FOR USING TESTS**</td></tr>
<tr><td>**If** . . . .</td><td>**USE** . . .</td></tr>
<tr><td>**V1 = NOMINAL (2) and**
V2 = INTERVAL/RATIO</td><td>**T TEST FOR 2 MEANS**</td></tr>
<tr><td>**V1 = NOMINAL (3+) and**
V2 = INTERVAL/RATIO</td><td>**ANOVA**</td></tr>
<tr><td>**V1 = NOMINAL and**
V2 = NOMINAL</td><td>**CHI SQUARE**</td></tr>
<tr><td>**V1 = INTERVAL/RATIO and**
V2 = INTERVAL/RATIO</td><td>**CORRELATION**</td></tr>
<tr><td>**V1 = INTERVAL/RATIO**</td><td>**T TEST FOR 1 MEAN**</td></tr>
</table>

Although the hypotheses are formulated, the data collected and tabulated, and *then* the tests are applied, it is important to understand the relationship of measurement scales and statistical tests in order to state the hypothesis in an accurate, testable format.

The sections in PART 2 explain how to "state the hypothesis."

PART 2

FORMULATING HYPOTHESES

These are the steps in formulating your hypotheses:

1. **A Research Design** identifying the dependent variable and all independent variables to be included in the study.
2. *Research questions*: formulating research questions: what you are interested in finding out about the variables from your research.
3. *Operational definitions*: defining each variable in terms of a) what elements or aspects it encompasses; b) how it will be *quantified.*
4. *Measuring the variables*:
   a) determining the measurement scale that will be most appropriate to "tap" the variable
   b) formulating the question for the questionnaire.
5. *Hypotheses statements*: determining the type of hypothesis to use for each of the research questions (based on the measurement scale used) and stating the hypothesis in terms of the statistical test to be used.

You have already done steps 1 - 4. This section will illustrate step 5: how to formulate and state statistically testable hypotheses.

Hypotheses are predictions. When you *hypothesize*, you are making an *inference*. A hypothesis is an *assumption* about something. It is generally understood as an assumption to be argued, or proved, or tested somehow. It is used in research as an assumption or prediction about a population. Since it is based on a *sample* of the population, it is tested *statistically* in order to determine whether the sample really is representative of the population.

A *hypothesis* makes a statement
about the *population*

In steps 1-4 you determined the variables that will be included in your study, and you determined their relationships in terms of dependent and independent variables. When you set up your research design, you indicated, both graphically and narratively, that relationship.

> You set up a *theory* about values and relationships
> of those variables as they exist in your *population*.

Since you intend to survey a sample rather than the entire population, you will make statements (hypotheses) about the population--statements that you will test statistically.

Statistics will tell you whether your statements about the population are valid.

Anyone looking at your research design can see, actually, what you are hypothesizing. However, your research must include the specific hypothesis statements along with your design, and later it must include the tests and test results applied to each statement.

If you look back at your research questions, you will notice that you are interested in values and relationships of the variables of your population:

(1) value: what is the mean of the population research grade?
(2) relationship: are male grades and female grades different? did classification make a difference?
(3) dependence: are"study" and "gender" dependent on one another?
(4) relationship: did grades go down as number of semester hours carried went up?

You will now formulate these values and relationships into *statistically testable* hypotheses. As preparation to do this, you'll do two things:

You'll start by using the following terminology for (1)-(4) above.

(1) the *mean* of a population
(2) *a difference of means* (mean male grade vs mean female grade)
(3) the *independence* of variables (study and gender)
(4) the *correlation* of variables (grades and semester hours)

You'll review various types of statistical tests. Learning the terminology and reviewing a few selected statistical tests will help you to formulate and state the hypotheses correctly.

STATING THE HYPOTHESES

Earlier in this unit you developed a research design showing the variables you selected for your research study. You then expressed the relationships you were predicting by asking research questions. You will now simply express those questions in the form of hypotheses.

A hypothesis is a prediction. Instead of asking (RQ 1)
"What is the mean research grade of all students who have taken research in the last two semesters?" we will state it in the form of a hypothesis--a *prediction*: the mean grade is -----. You will then *test* the prediction.

In order to test a prediction statistically, you must state it in a precise way and *make very clear what variables are involved.*

OK. Let's state your prediction:
   The mean research grade is 80 or higher (≥ 80).

HERE IS A STATISTICAL BULLETIN:!!!

   You don't test your prediction.
   You test the *opposite* of your prediction!

The hypothesis that says the opposite of what you are predicting is the
null hypothesis (Ho)

The Null Hypothesis

It is more scientific to apply the statistical test to the *opposite* of your prediction, to try to *disprove* the opposite. (Some statisticians refer to this as "the good sport theory.") If you can disprove the opposite, then your prediction was right.

 This "opposite" hypothesis is referred to as the *null* hypothesis and is indicated this way:

Ho   The mean research grade is less than 8o (< 80)

IMPORTANT!! Test the Null Hypothesis

If the null hypothesis is disproved (*rejected*), then you accept your research (*alternate*) hypothesis. From now on you will refer to the hypotheses as *null* and *alternate*. (You can also refer to the alternate as the *research* hypothesis). They will be indicated as:

Ho (null) and HA (alt). You can also "number" the hypothesis: H1 or HO1

A hypothesis includes the variable or variables whose relationship is to be tested. You will notice, however, that H1 contains only one variable; you are simply predicting the data on one variable. This will require a univariate (one variable) test. If you refer back to the table at the end of the Operational Definitions, showing "shorthand for using tests," you will see that for a univariate test we will use the ONE SAMPLE T TEST, or T TEST FOR 1 MEAN.

H 1 TESTING WORKSHEET

Variable 1: research grade　　　　　**Meas scale: Ratio**
Type of test: One Sample T Test

The hypothesis for a one variable test can be stated this way:

Ho The mean research grade is less than 80 (<80)
H1 The mean research grade is 80 or greater than 80 (≥ 80)

The rest of your hypotheses (RQ 2 - 8) will require *bivariate* tests--two variable tests. In each you will be testing relationships. Note that these were the questions asked in your research design.

The null always says that there is no relationship: there is no correlation--or, there is no difference. Or to put it another way: the correlation is zero--the difference is zero.

RQ 2: Was there a difference between male and female research grades?

Of course you are predicting that there is a difference. If you don't think there is a relationship with an independent variable, do not include it in your research design.

H 2 TESTING WORKSHEET

Variable 1: gender	Meas scale: NOM - 2 samples
Variable 2: grade	Meas scale: RATIO

Type of test: Two Sample T Test (See note below)

The hypothesis for a two sample test can be stated this way:

> **H0 There is no difference between male and female research grades.**
> **H2 There is a difference between male and female research grades.**

IMPORTANT NOTE

The DV is the research grade (a "mean" measurement)

The "difference" is between *the two groups*, or samples, created by the IV (gender). We called it a T Test for Two Means; SPSS calls this the Two Sample T test. SPSS refers to "groups" as "samples."

→ Note that the difference is NOT between grades and gender. It's the difference *in* grades *between* male and female.

It is important to state each hypothesis in a simple, correct way that actually makes clear what type of test will be used to test it. For each type of test to be used, therefore, there is usually a more or less standard way of stating the hypotheses. Until you obtain a real familiarity and facility for these typical hypotheses formats, it will help to

- ☞ study each of these "hypothesis testing worksheet" boxes carefully
- ☞ study the format of the hypothesis based on the information in the box
- ☞ use the hypothesis "worksheets" below

The worksheet brings together the *precise variables*, the *measurement scale* to be used to tap the variable, and the *type of test* to be used. This will help you to state the hypothesis correctly.

RQ 3: Did the research grade differ according to the students' majors?

H 3 TESTING WORKSHEET

Variable 1: major   Meas. Scale: NOM - 4 samples
Variable 2: grade   Meas. Scale: RATIO
Type of Test: ONE WAY ANOVA--F TEST

> Ho Major did not make a difference in the research grade.
> H3 The research grade differed depending on major.
>   (or: Major made a difference in the research grade.)

ANOVA—the FTest is used when a nominal variable has more than two categories (populations).

RQ4: Did the total number of semester hours a student carried during the semester the research was taken influence the research grade?

H 4 TESTING WORKSHEET

Variable 1: sem hrs   Meas. Scale: RATIO
Variable 2: grade   Meas. Scale: RATIO
Type of Test: Pearson's Correlation Coefficient

> **Ho There is no correlation between semester hours carried and the research grade.**
> **H4 There is a correlation between semester hours carried and the research grade.**

RQ 5: Was there a correlation between how much time the student spent studying for the course and what the research grade was?

H5 TESTING WORKSHEET

Variable 1: study   Meas. Scale: NOM - 4
Variable 2: grade   Meas. Scale: RATIO
Type of Test: ONE WAY ANOVA--F TEST ** See note

> Ho   The time spent studying for the course did not make a difference in the research grade.
>
> H5   The research grade differed depending on the time spent studying for the course.

** NOTE: *ARE YOU CONFUSED?*
WHY DID THE RQ ASK ABOUT A CORRELATION, BUT *THE TEST BEING USED IS ANOVA?*

At the time of the research questions you were simply asking about relationships on your research design and you thought of "study" as quantitative . . . something like numbers of hours, etc. When you did the OPERATIONAL DEFINITION, however, you decided that putting hours in "categories" would get more honest answers. So you gave STUDY a NOMINAL measurement. As you can see in the types of statistical tests, you can't do a correlation hypothesis when one of the variables is measured with categories. Only ratio and interval scales can be correlated—Hyp 5 has to be tested as a *difference of means.*

RQ 6: Was there an association between how interested in statistics the student was and the student's research grade?

** NOTE: The RQ is stated in general terms. The way that the variables were measured will determine what type of test to use.

H6 TESTING WORKSHEET

Variable 1: interest   Meas. Scale: INTERVAL
Variable 2: grade   Meas. Scale: RATIO
Type of Test: Pearson's Correlation Coefficient

> Ho   There is no correlation between interest in statistics and the research grade.
>
> H6   There is a correlation between interest in statistics and the research grade.

RQ 7: Were Marketing majors "more interested" in learning research than other majors?

Simply
for
Kids!

AuthorHouse™
1663 Liberty Drive
Bloomington, IN 47403
www.authorhouse.com
Phone: 1-800-839-8640

First published by AuthorHouse   12/01/2011

ISBN: 978-1-4634-3048-1 (sc)

Printed in the United States of America

Simply for Kids!

By Will Davis

authorHOUSE®

CONTENTS

SPRING!

By Will Davis

The snow was melting!
The green grass was visible again!
Summer was coming,
But this was really spring.
It was warm again.
As we shed our heavy coats.
Mom and Dad, of course,
Would loudly object.
Because it was not warm enough.
The birds and the squirrels,
Had finally returned.
We knew this because of their chatter,
And beaughtiful, sweet songs
Could quite plainly, be heard.
It was time for those outdoor sports,
That we all loved so.
Baseball! Fishing! Biking! Hiking!
How we missed them so!
The trees with their buds,
Showing traces of green,
While the flowers prepared,
To dance with the wind,
Just like royal queens.
Dipping and bowing their heads,
In recognition of the coming of the green!
The boys and their young ladies,
Practicing, when they thought
No one could see,
What spring really meant for you and me,
As we embraced each other,
Very close and quite tightly!
While riding the roller coaster,
That some of us thought was true love!

SUMMER!

By Will Davis

School is out!
It's over with!
Summer vacation is here!
We have survived
The shut-up, pent-up
Desire to roam about free!
Digging up worms for fishing,
Maybe even teasing the girls,
So they would notice me!
What if the other guys
Were to catch me and see
ME kissing the girls in glee?
Going for bicycle rides,
With no place in mind.
Just cruising around
To see what wonders we could find.
Stopping at the old horse trough
For a drink of water or two.
Playing games of hide and seek,
About our small town.
The girls would join in our fun,
But we didn't mind.
The more kids there were,
The more fun we had,
During our vacation time!

AUTUMN

By Will Davis

I would wonder about the mystery of fall;
Why the leaves would change colors and all.
I was told by others that thought they knew.
The leaves had to fall to make room for those that are new.
When the weather grew cold, the leaves would fall.
But before they fell, they would change colors for all.
The green would change to red, yellow, gold, and brown.
Then they would let go of the tree and fall to the ground.
I would have to rake them up into piles.
It was hard work for a little one like me.
But then I would get to have some fun,
As I would get to jump into the pile joyfully!
My dad would come out with a stern look upon his face.
He would scold me quite heartily and put me in my place.
Then I would rake the leaves into piles again,
So me, my brother, and sisters could jump into the pile again.
Soon our fun and games were finally over.
Again we had to rake the leaves into a pile.
Dad would bring big bags out to put the leaves in.
Our fun was over, but in a few days we got to do it all over again!

WINTER!*

By Will Davis

I remember, as a child,
How I wondered at
The snow drifting down,
Covering, with white
All that was around.
How, as children,
We couldn't wait
To go out and build a snowman
That looked like a clown.
The time we spent
Looking for just the right look;
The right size carrot for the nose,
The old scarf, from where? No one knows.
We did not have a top hat,
So we used an old bag
That was dirty and brown.
Set it upon his head for a crown.
Tree twigs for his arms.
Old gloves for hands, we found.
For his eyes, we used black coal.
For a mouth, an old, flattened tin can
That made him look quite stern.
Everything was just right.
Then would come our snowball fight.
Covered in snow, wet, cold, and shivering,
We would come inside, quivering.
A hot chocolate and wrapped in a warm blanket,
While we huddled next to the old warm, wood stove.
Drinking our hot chocolate
And listening to winter music.
And best of all, the Christmas carols,
To make us all happy and toasty warm,
Waiting for Santa Claus,
And the white Christmas to come!

SKIPPING SCHOOL!

By Will Davis

I remember one cold winter day,
My brother and I wanted to play.
So we decided, from school,
We would play hooky!
Everything went as planned.
We walked to school as usual,
But on the way, we made a detour.
Thinking that we would not be caught,
If we stayed away from the streets.
We wandered about the neighborhood,
Sneaking from one backyard to another,
Until we came upon the great river.
We followed the river for many long moments,
Watching the pieces if ice flow by,
Tumbling along in the bouncing current.
We threw snowballs at the ice,
Keeping score of the hits and misses.
We had no idea of the passage of time.
Soon, we decided it was time to go home.
We believed we had spent the entire day
Playing about the neighborhood and on the river.
Boy! Were we ever wrong about the passage of time!
To our dismay, when we got home, we discovered
That our day-long excursion was only two hours.
There was a great clamor when we entered the house.
We were quite cold from our adventure.
Our parents stared at us quite sternly.
Then they administered our punishment quite appropriately.
To bed we were sent, with our bottoms warmed quite nicely.
Here ends our tale of skipping school.
Don't do it, if you know what's good for you.
Because, if you're caught, your punishment will be the rule!

UGH!

By Will Davis

I went to the bathroom the other day.
Everything was fine and went my way.
The whole event went very well,
As all that was in—I did expel!
Unfortunately, for me, you see,
Good luck wasn't meant to be.
As everyone could tell by the smell,
For me, it did not really go that well.
It seems that in my great haste,
From my body to expel my waste,
I sat upon the seat and forgot one little item!
And with great ease, my pants, I did fill them!

THE LITTLE MOUSE!

By Will Davis

I was up late this weekend day,
To the kitchen, I made my way.
Put the coffee pot to boil;
In the fry pan, I put some oil.
Put bread in the toaster to brown.
Still upon my face there was a frown.
Something didn't look quite right.
For right there in plain sight,
My coffee cup was standing upright.
I usually put it away upside down.
I must have forgotten, for I found
In a spot, that was unusual
There was a tiny black thread
Dangling from the top.
This was quite unusual.
Not sure just as to what it was,
I peeked inside, not disturbing the cup.
Inside, on the bottom, was a big black blob.
I did not touch it, for I knew
As soon as I saw it, I knew what to do.
I got a saucer from the cupboard above, and
Placed it on the top of that coffee mug.
Trapped inside, as safe as he could be,
Was this little mouse that came to visit me.
He was as cute as he could be.
Curled into a tight little ball,
Sleeping so soundly, and so peacefully.
I could do nothing, but let it be;
In spite of this compulsive revulsion, inside of me.
As I continued to prepare to feed me,
I knew as I ate, that it could not,
Should not, remain with me.
While that little mouse slept so soundly,
I pondered what must truly be.
Of course, for sure, he had to go!
I took him out to the back alley,
And with little ceremony, set him free!

THE MATTRESS TAG!

By Will Davis

When I was just a snip of a lad,
I often wondered about mattress tags.
I asked my parents one day,
Why I should not take off that tag.
They showed me the printing upon it.
I read in my own little way,
"DO NOT REMOVE UNDER,
PENALTY OF THE LAW!"
"What does that mean?" I asked my paw.
He said quite jokingly,
"They will come and get you!
And take you very far away.
In a dark room with no windows,
They will definitely put you!
They'll feed you bread and water,
For the rest of your days.
You will have to wear the same clothes,
Day after day after day after day!
Forever and ever you will be,
Locked up and never set free!
You will never see Mommy and me,
Ever, never, and forever again!"
I was scared out of my wits,
And promised I would leave
That little white tag alone.
With that fear, he made me believe.
One day there was a great commotion.
At the front door, there was a lot of motion.
When through that door there came a huge package.
With two men in control,
Into the bedroom went the huge baggage.
I watched with curiosity,
And a great deal of wonder,
As the outer covering of that package
Was completely torn asunder.

When all had been removed completely,
There standing on its end,
Stood a spanking brand new mattress,
With fancy stitching end to end.
I marveled at the intricate design,
As the pattern swirled and intertwined.
I was surely hoping and praying,
That this new mattress would be mine.
Then I saw it! I could not turn away.
That little white tag
Looked as big as a bale of hay!
I could not help myself,
And took a hold of it.
I did not mean for it to be torn away!
I just wanted to see what it looked like.
Did not see as the men took the mattress away.
Instinctively, I grabbed that little white tag.
Because of curiosity, I wanted to see what it had to say!
When the mattress was moved away,
I instinctively tightened my grip,
Upon that teeny, tiny white tag.
Watched in horror as it was ripped away!
Just then, into the room stepped my dad.
"What's in your hand?" he asked sternly,
As I knelt on the floor with that damned tag!
"What did I tell you about that mattress tag?"
He addressed me in a voice that was very stern!
"Now you will have to go away!" he said,
"Until your lesson, you have learned!"
He had not forgotten from the other day, what he had said.
The evening meal went as expected.
I hardly ate a thing, as was expected.
Went to bed that night with the light on!
Lay awake for what seemed like an eon!
Then with a screaming and a wailing,
The lights went out with that eerie sound.
It was an air raid drill that I knew not of.
I screamed in terror as I dove under the bed.
Crawled to the furthest corner under the bed!
Trembled in terror as the sirens sounded.
When down the hallway I could hear,
The sound of heavy footsteps,

That, in me, put a great fear!
I scrunched myself into that corner as far as I could.
Listened as those heavy footfalls came near.
They were coming to get me, I was quite sure!
As those pounding feet came through the door!

H 7 TESTING WORKSHEET

Variable 1: major
Variable 2: interest
Type of Test: _____

Meas. Scale: NOM - 4
Meas. Scale: INTERVAL
(see discussion below)

(read this)

The hypothesis testing information above would indicate a multiple sample test (ONE WAY ANOVA) since we have a *difference of means* (interest levels for the various majors) and since there are *more than two* categories.

But the RQ is interested in "marketing" majors vs the other majors. That would make two categories. Even though your questionnaire will have four categories, for this particular hypothesis, you will simply use the marketing majors as one category and all the other majors (combined) as a second category. Then you will need a two sample test (TWO SAMPLE T TEST). Fill in the type of test above.

> **Ho There is no difference between marketing majors interest in statistics and other majors interest in statistics.**
> **H7 There is a difference between marketing majors interest in statistics and other majors interest in statistics.**

RQ 8 Was there a difference in study time between male students and female students?

H 8 TESTING WORKSHEET

Variable 1: gender
Variable 2: study
Type of Test: Chi Square

Meas. Scale: NOM - 2
Meas. Scale: NOM - 4

> **Ho The variables of gender and study are independent**
> **H8 The variables of gender and study are RELATED.**

When both variables are measured by the nominal scale, the test cannot be a "means" test. Chi Square compares "numbers of frequencies" in the categories to see whether the variables are independent of each other or whether they are influencing one another.

YOU NOW HAVE 8 TESTABLE HYP0THESES! Study the "hypothesis testing" worksheet boxes above and compare to the test tables at the end of Operational Definitions to see how the measurement scale and the type of test must "fit" since different tests are designed for different measurements.

TAKE A BREAK . . . CLEAR YOUR HEAD . . . COME BACK AND REVIEW WHATEVER YOU DON'T UNDERSTAND.

STUDY THE TWO INSERTS ON THE VARIABLES "STUDY" AND "INTEREST" (next 2 pages).

The next step is to develop a valid questionnaire to collect the data.

INSERT 1

 This insert is not meant to confuse you but to show you the thinking that should go into tapping the variable in the most reasonable way.

THE VARIABLE "STUDY"

Remember that in the "research questions" you decided that "study" means how much time the student spent studying for the course.
Notice that this is a quantitative variable: numbers. But here you have to consider some things before deciding on the measurement scale.

The most important consideration is how to collect the most reliable information from the respondent. If a student took research two semesters ago, will the student remember (recall) the real time devoted to research? Even if a student does remember (vividly, because it was so much work?), will the student know how to relay the data—hours—days—etc? Or perhaps the student will do a bit of "fabrication"—either overstate or understate the actual time spent. The most important consideration is that all the students deal more or less with the same question.

When you have these types of considerations with tapping a variable, it's often best to use the nominal scale—categories—for them to check. Which turns it into a nominal measurement.

Question on Survey
How many hours per week did you study for research?
0 ___   2-3 ___   4-6 ___   7-9 ___   10 or more ___

THE VARIABLE "INTEREST IN STATISTICS"

"Interest" does not have any inherent numerical value. It is important to 1) show exactly what you mean by this variable; and 2) how you intend to quantify it. You could leave it as you have it: an interval scale where the respondent simply circles a number to say how interested he/she is. However, you'll get a better idea if you try to formulate questions that are as "behavioral" as possible. That is, try to get evidence that you can measure.

Let's decide that (1) students who like statistics and did well will have more "interest" in the research course; and (2) students who believed that they will need to know research for their careers will have more "interest" in the course. Not fool proof but somewhat better.

Now, since you have two factors, you also need to determine how you will combine them: you have to get *one measurement* for interest. You can approach this by asking the question in category form BUT give weights to the categories and average them out. That is, you'll consider the categories in both questions below as 1 (low); 2 (middle); and 3 (high). Then we can average the two categories checked by the student (the two "weights") and have one number to represent "interest". See no. 5 and no. 6 on the questionnaire that follows. When you code your tally sheet, these two questions will be treated like two interval scales which you will average to get one number.

You might think "why go to all that trouble?" Depends how important your research is. I'm showing you various ways to tap a variable.

PART 3

COLLECTING THE DATA

THE QUESTIONNAIRE

This survey will be done with a questionnaire given to students who have taken the research course.

The questionnaire must be designed to collect data on the variables included in your hypotheses. In order to test the hypotheses, you must tap the relevant variables in order to get a "measurement" on each variable. The hypotheses were based on the research questions and on the *measurements* in the *operational definitions*. Therefore, you can base your questions on the operational definitions as well.

You must be careful to state the questions in such a way that the "respondent" will know precisely what you are asking and know the format in which to respond. Here are some reminders about formulating your questions:

> Avoid the "double barrel" (only one question at a time)
> Avoid "leading" with biased language
> Avoid "leading" with questions that have social implications if answered a certain way
> Avoid asking for data that will be hard to recall

In short, you want two things:
    . . . everyone to answer as honestly and correctly as possible
    . . . everyone to interpret the question in the same way

Develop your questionnaire as carefully as possible; it is your instrument for collecting the data. And you want the data you collect to reflect as accurately as possible the data of the sample.

NOTE: It is not a bad idea to "TEST" your questionnaire on someone in your sample who will give you honest feedback where he/she had a problem knowing what you want.

QUESTIONNAIRE

Hi! I'm doing a study for my business research class that includes students who have taken the course. If you have taken the course in the last two years (Spring 98 or Spring 99), please take a minute to complete this questionnaire. Your answers are strictly anonymous--do include your name.

Thanks a lot. ☺ ❀ ❁ _ ❋ _

1. Please check one: Male ___ Female ___

2. Please indicate your major by checking *one* category.

   CIS ___   MGT ___   ACCT ___   MGT ___

3. How many semester hours did you carry *during the semester* in which you took business research? _____ Sem Hrs

4. To the best of your knowledge, how many hours a week did you spend studying *for the business research course*?

   0-2 ___   3-6 ___   7-10 ___   11 or more ___ hrs per wk

5. What grade did you make in your statistics course?

   A or B ___   C ___   D or lower ___

6. When you were taking the course, how likely did you think it was that you would use business research in your future career? (Check only one)

   Very likely ___   Somewhat likely ___   Not likely ___

7. What was your final grade in research?
   Please give the numerical average: (e.g., 82) _____

DATA PREPARATION AND TALLY

Editing the Data

The first thing to do, after your questionnaires are returned, is to look through them and see whether they are "complete" enough to use. An occasional omitted question doesn't mean you have to eliminate a questionnaire; however, if too many questions have been left blank, it is probably best to eliminate the whole questionnaire.

Next, determine whether you have the number of questionnaires that you want. Perhaps you have too many. Or perhaps you are intending to do a "stratified" sample and want equal or proportionate numbers in the various groups. If you want to eliminate questionnaires on the basis of number or strata, be sure to do it in an "unbiased" way. In other words, pull them *at random*, without any reference to responses.

Next, it's a good idea to stack the questionnaires and number them in the upper right hand corner. You may get interrupted while tallying your data, and the numbers help to keep things in order. Also, each one of the questionnaires now represents a "respondent" or "observation." For example, questionnaire No.1 is OBS 1.

CODING THE VARIABLES

Now that your questionnaires are back, you must do several things to "manage" your data. The first of these is *coding* the variables.

The only way you can count, measure, or test data for purposes of analysis is to quantify it. The only way the statistical software can run tests is with numbers. Therefore, everything has to be coded numerically.

Some variables (quantitative variables) are already in numerical form. Your DV of "semester grade" for example is a number. The variable "semester hours" is a number. And Nos. 5 and 6 are interval scale numbers—but see the inserts. You have to find a way of combining the two scales.

Question No. 1 is a variable measured nominally: Give each category a number: e.g. Males as "1" and Females as "2"

Questions No. 2 and 4 are measured nominally: give each category a number, beginning with 1 and so on.

Since Questions 5 and 6 together will give you "interest," you have to get one numerical value for each observation (OBS). For each OBS the mean of Q5 andQ6 is the number on the tally sheet. [good hint: If you have several items for a variable, one way to handle it is to have a column for each on the tally sheet, record each in its column, and follow with an average column that will be the measurement numbers for the variable.]

TALLYING THE DATA

1. On a spread sheet label the first column "OBS" and list the individual OBS down the first column *by number.* NOTE: make sure the people in your sample do not identify themselves in any way—all OBS must be anonymous. See Prof. M's note at the top of the questionnaire.

2. Determine an abbreviated form of each variable and insert at the top of the columns, starting with Q 1.

3. Under the variable name insert the measurement scale.

4. Fill in the data given by the OBS.

IMPORTANT
You need one measure for each variable on your framework.

You can tally your data by hand on a columnar spreadsheet, or on an Excel spreadsheet. SPSS will import Excel. SPSS for Windows is a familiar software used in research—more on that later.

PART 4

THEORETICAL DISTRIBUTIONS AND LOOKING FOR SIGNIFICANCE

THEORETICAL DISTRIBUTIONS

If you have ever taken a statistics course, you learned about getting a "feel for the data." Or perhaps you collected data on a given subject for your boss or team and you had the job of presenting it in an orderly manner. You probably used measures of *central tendency* (mean, median, mode, frequency distributions etc) and even perhaps measures of *dispersion* (range, standard deviation and variance). In order to make the data more accessible you may have created graphs and pie charts for your Power Point presentation. You presented a "feel for the data" that was obtained from actual raw data, from *empirical* distributions. In other words, the data was obtained through primary research--collected from an actual sample.

This section will present a review, or overview, of *theoretical* distributions. Theoretical distributions will enable you to make certain predictions about a population based on data you gathered from a sample of the population. For example, you work in the office of a large Honda agency and your boss gives you this assignment: "Do some research on the preferences of females vs males when they're looking at a new car. We'll present your findings to the sales department." So you do the research on a sample of females and males as they come in, you prepare a Power Point presentation with a "feel for the data" (graphs, etc.), you formulate and test the proper hypotheses, and you say to the sales persons, "I found a significant difference in 10 out of 12 areas in what females want in a new car vs what males want."

Notice the word "significant." We throw that phrase around a lot. But if someone in your audience says "Do you mean statistically significant?" You will be able to say "yes, I measured the differences in perceived importance of these twelve items (on the screen) and in each case except music and GPS the perceived importance was significantly different for males and females at the .05 level." That's what you'll be able to say if you persevere through this section.

We'll assume you know nothing about statistical testing and present a very simplified overview of finding significance—scientific significance. This overview is intended for the "non-research" person in the firm who is asked to research something. It is for anyone who just can't remember what he/she learned in the statistics course and wants to do some credible research.

In order to find significance we first have to look at the *theoretical* distribution, called also the *normal* distribution. A large population will be "normally" distributed in many of its characteristics. If you plot the scores of characteristics, such as age, or height, or amount spent for movies, of a large enough number of people, you will get a "normal" distribution. If you plot those characteristics by *mean* and *standard deviation,* the distribution will be *symmetrical*—it will be a *bell curve.*

The *majority* will be in the *middle*.
The *few* will be in the *extremes* on either end.

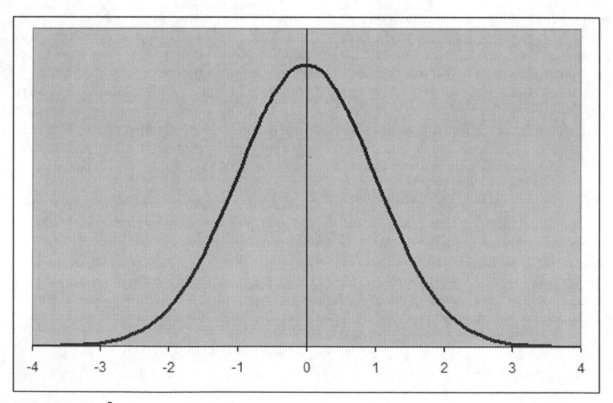

Distribution A

The mean is set at zero (we don't know what is being plotted). The numbers on the X axis are standard deviations (distances from the mean).

DORCAS MLADENKA

Chance occurrences of most characteristics in nature will be described by the normal distribution. This is the law of averages. This is the law of *large* numbers. This is the law of *probability.* Normal distributions are everywhere! stock market fluctuations; yearly rainfall; NBA scores; and blood pressure readings. It has been established that the mean for blood pressure is 85 mm and the standard deviation is 20 mm.

B

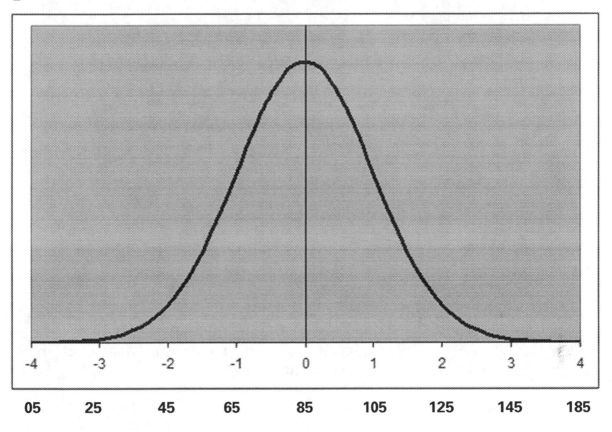

| 05 | 25 | 45 | 65 | 85 | 105 | 125 | 145 | 185 |

Normal Distribution of Blood Pressure Readings

The mean is in the center—where most readings would be found: around the mean of 85. Readings of 20 mm lower and 20 mm higher would be 65 and 105 respectively. Look at the extremes on either side of the mean: Time for medical help, right? We'll see later on how few, relatively speaking, that would be in a population. [Can we say it? The poor folks on either end die?] Remember these are percentages of large numbers.

Let's do another one. If you plot the IQ of everyone in the U.S., for example, most people's scores will fall around the *average* IQ. It has been established that the IQ mean is 100 and that IQ is distributed normally with a standard deviation of 15. There will be fewer scores on the low end and fewer scores on the high end. Most (68%) will be in the middle—on either side of the mean—from 85 to 115.

C

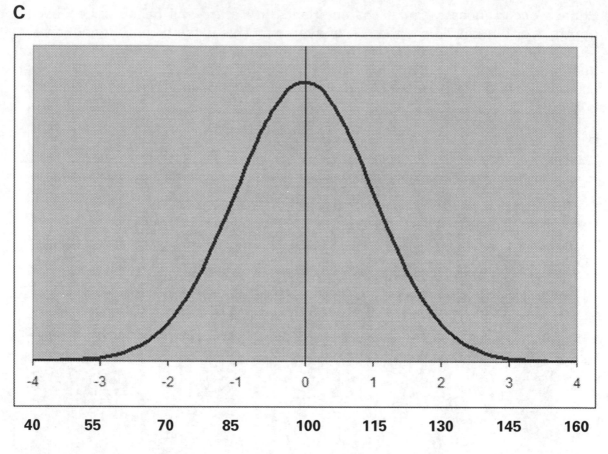

| 40 | 55 | 70 | 85 | 100 | 115 | 130 | 145 | 160 |

Normal Distribution of IQs

Where did 68% come from? It's the area from -1 to + 1 standard deviations under the curve. Let's look now at areas under the curve.

D

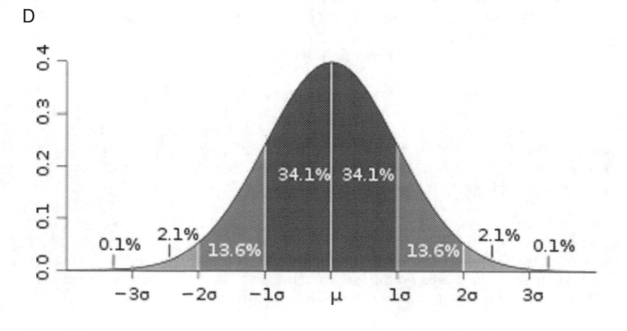

In the center of a distribution we have μ (mu), the mean of a population. Along the x axis we have σ (lower case sigma) standard deviations of a population. We can see that one standard deviation above and below the mean is 34.1% + 34.1% (68.4%) of the population. The distribution is showing us that 68% of any *normal distribution* is within one standard deviation of the mean—half above and half below.

Study this:

In the IQ example of Distribution C above, showing IQ distribution, half the population falls between 100 and 85 and half falls between 100 and 115 IQ.

Within two standard deviations (-2 and +2) 13.6% + 13.6% are added to 68.4% to show that 95.6% of the population has an IQ from 70 to 130 (check it out on the distribution above).

Adding the third standard deviation (2.1 below and 2.1 above) includes 99.8% of the population. On the high end you would have people with an IQ of 145 plus and of course 55 or below on the low end.

Then answer this:

What percentage of the population has an IQ over 130?

ANSWER (Don't Look until you try)

> An IQ of 130 is two standard deviations above the mean
> The area that two sds cover is 95%
> But that 95% covers *both* sides of the mean
> That leaves 2.5% above the second sd and 2.5% below
> So only 2.5% of the population has an IQ over 130

The areas under the curve are defined by the probability of an event—expressed in percentages. If a score falls within the area form 0 to+1, the mathematical probability that the score would fall there is 34%. Or, to put it another way, it is probable that 34% of the scores in a normal distribution will fall within one deviation above the mean of a population.

Suppose you know your IQ is 110 and you want to "locate" yourself on the normal distribution. Since you know the standard deviation for IQ, your can use a **z score** to locate yourself under the normal curve.

Z SCORES

Measurements aren't always easy to compare. For example. a student received a score of 75 on an English test. The mean of the class was 69, the sd 12. The same student received a score of 93 on a biology test. The class mean was 90, the sd 3. On which test did the student have the better score when compared with the class?

We need a common yardstick, and we can get this by referring to the normal distribution. When the scores are converted for sd units, the sd becomes the common yardstick, and comparisons can be made. Such converted scores are called z scores or *standard scores*.

> The z score takes a raw score (e.g., a test grade, an IQ) and changes it to a standard score.

> A z score is the number of standard deviations that a score is above or below the mean. The formula for converting a raw score into a z score is:

$$Z = \frac{\text{Raw Score} - \text{Mean of Distribution}}{\text{Standard Deviation of Distribution}}$$

LOOKING FOR SIGNIFICANCE

Let's get back to your presentation to the sales force at the Honda dealership. You told them that the perceived importance of ten out of twelve features was "significantly" different between males and females. You assured them that you meant statistically significant at the "05 level." What exactly does that mean. Well, when we talk about the areas (%age of occurrences) under the curve, we're talking about probability. Remember? The "law of averages"—the law of large numbers—the law of probability. What is the probability that someone will have an IQ between 100 and 115? The probability is 34.1%. What is the probability that someone will have an IQ between 85 and 115? The probability is 68%.

Are you suspecting where this is going in terms of significance? Simply put, the software will solve a two sample T test equation for you and give you a Z score—a standard score. (Thank God for software!—it does the number crunching for us.) It looks at the perceived means of females vs males and the difference of females means vs male means. It looks at the size of your sample. And it gives you a Z score which will tell you where, on a normal distribution, the "found" difference in your sample falls under the curve.

Where would you *wish* it would fall—close to the mean? In the area of probability? Chance? Not really. If you're trying to show the sales persons that women have different priorities about car features than men, you want the difference to be due to the *variable* (gender) rather than probability.

Let's repeat this because it is the *essence* of hypothesizing and doing credible research.

Your goal, in testing your hypotheses, is to be able to "infer" from the sample to the population. To do that you must determine whether a difference or a correlation indicated by a statistical test is due to probability or due to the independent variables of your research design. Is the difference or correlation "real" or is it "chance"?

Certainly you can observe some patterns and differences just by looking at your tally sheet—or even better—looking at the feel for the data that you might have prepared. What you can't observe looking at the raw data is whether you can make inferences about the population based on this raw data from a small sample.

The question, then, would be *how* different must the differences be?

Well, since you've looked at areas under the curve, you have an idea where you would like that Z score to fall: not within one standard deviation of the mean—that's too probable. How about two standard deviations within the mean. That includes 95% of the variables under study. If we can get beyond two standard deviations from the mean, we'd be in the 5% area. If we're at NASA testing something on the shuttle, we'd want to be more *picky* than that—perhaps in the 1% area. In the world of business, and most social sciences, we're going for the ".05" area. We reject a null score that falls farther from the mean than the 95% level. We refer to the area of rejection as the .05 level and indicate it like this:

$$p = < .05$$

The area of probability ends at the .05 level. Anything beyond the .05 level is in the **critical** area—the area of **significance**. What you're asking is this: is the difference or correlation due to chance—is it probable—or is it real—due to the variable involved? The statistical term for a relationship that is due, not to chance, but to your prediction about the variable, is **significance**. You can say the difference is "statistically significant."

Significance means
"beyond the area of probability"

PART 5

COMPLETING YOUR OWN
RESEARCH PROJECT

Congratulations. You are now ready to complete a research project of your own. With your own subject and variables, the sample project gives you much room to formulate your own hypotheses in the same manner. You should have a research design or research questions showing your reader what variables you are testing. The sample has given you numerous ways to tap the variables with a survey. Follow all the steps throughout the workbook and you can "theorize" and "test" any variables you think are relevant. There is so much more material in statistical testing that we didn't include here; however, with the tests we did look at, you have a broad spectrum of testing to use. Be sure not to skip the steps of measurement scales and operational definitions of your variables, otherwise you will truly be on a slippery slope when you get to the point of testing your hypotheses.

You are now ready to run the tests. Since I cannot be there to look over you shoulder and prompt you, you'll have to run it on your own; however, there are so many aids you can use. As I noted above, businesses, universities, and libraries are good sources for SPSS software. It is menu driven and easy to follow if you read the directions carefully. I also suggest going to Amazon books, enter SPSS, and you will find all sorts of SPSS for Dummies etc.—books that can help you use the software. SPSS will perform descriptive statistics for you since you will have input the data from your questionnaires.

Part 5 includes the following miscellaneous notes that pertain to doing statistical research but which were purposely omitted in the design above in order to keep it simple and easy to follow. At this point however you should look at them in order to enhance your understanding of looking for significance.

Directional and Non-directional Hypotheses

Professor M's hypothesis about male and female grades was simply predicting a difference (between males and females), not which would be higher. That difference could fall on either side of the mean, and this is referred to as a *non directional* hypothesis. For significance, the *t value test* we would use would be a *two tail* test.

This means that it doesn't matter whether your test value is positive or negative—anything beyond 1.96 (the second deviation above or below the mean) would fall into the critical area (the significance area).

If the hypothesis predicted not only a difference, but a "direction" (e.g. males research grades > female research grades), the hypothesis is "directional" and requires s "one tail" test. If the test were a "one tail" test, the entire .05 area would be on one end of the distribution. The area of rejection would be larger, making it easier to obtain significance. The sample study made non directional hypotheses for two-tailed tests, making it harder to find significance and thus making for better research.

Special Distributions

Seeing where the test statistic falls tells whether we are in the critical area or not. However, we have to consider an important element. The distribution diagrams in Section4 were normal distributions based on large numbers. But when samples are based not on large numbers but on small distributions, does the critical area fall in the same place? Logic would tell one that the critical area (remember: the area where we can reject our null) will change depending on the size of the distribution. We would presume that it should be somewhat "harder" to get beyond the area of probability with small samples. And we would be right.

Statisticians have formulated a number of distributions for samples of small size. Instead of drawing a distribution curve for every possible score generated, these distributions are arranged in tables. When you run a T-test, therefore, you can refer to a t distribution table. If you tell the table what size your sample is and what your level of confidence is, it will tell you where the critical area begins.

With statistical software the test results give us "p" or "significance" whieh tells us whether we are in the .05 area. It isn't a bad idea, however, to use the tables a few times. You will see that the smaller the sample the farther away from the mean the critical area starts.

Notes on the Correlation Coefficient

We've talked about testing differences. Sometimes, however, we might hypothesize about relationships. For example:

a) as the mean of variable X goes up, the mean of variable Y goes up.
   or
b) as the mean of variable X goes up, the mean of variable Y goes down.

Example (a) is a positive correlation. Example (b) is a negative correlation.

It is important to note that correlation says nothing about *reasons* for the relationship.

Correlation is not the same as cause and effect. Correlation merely indicates a relationship.

There are three elements of correlation:

1. direction
2. magnitude
3. relationship

Examples (a) and (b) above show direction. Guilford's scale below shows magnitude (the strength of the relationship).

The index for correlation is called a coefficient and is symbolized by the letter "r" — called *Pearson's r.*

The index itself doesn't give us much sense of the magnitude of the correlation. A better sense of magnitude is obtained by what's called the **coefficient of determination.** This means simply squaring **r** to get a percentage of relationship: r^2

For example, if **r** = .50, this does not means a proportion of 50% correlation. Squaring r = 25% which is the proportion of variance that measures have in common.

GUILFORD'S GUIDE: A ROUGH GUIDE
TO CORRELATIOIN AND MAGNITUDE

COEFFICIENT (**R**)	CORRELATION	RELATIONSHIP
< .20	SLIGHT	ALMOST NEGLIGIBLE (E. G. R = .20; R^2 = 4%)
.20 - .40	LOW	DEFINITE BUT SMALL (E. G. R = .40; R^2 = 16%)
.40 - .70	MODERATE	SUBSTANTIAL (E. G. R = .70; R^2 = 49%)
.70 - .90	HIGH	MARKED (E. G. R = .90; R^2 = 81%)
> .90	VERY HIGH	VERY DEPENDABLE (E. G. R = .90; R^2 = > 90%)

THE GUILFORD SCALE GIVES YOU A WAY TO DESCRIBE YOUR CORRELATION

APPENDIX

OUTLINE AND NOTES
FOR A RESEARCH REPORT

(Title e.g.) WHAT WOMEN LOOK FOR IN THE PURCHASE OF A NEW CAR

INTRODUCTION

Anyone watching television today is aware of the number of car ads . . . . .

There has also been some new awareness of the purchasing power of women today . . . (refer to the cover of Time Magazine on "women are richer . . .")

LITERATURE SURVEY

(Some topics call for a survey of the literature . . . Previous studies . . . etc)
The Lit Survey tends to give you credibity . . . you are familiar with your topic

PROBLEM AREA (or RESEARCH QUESTIONS)

More women are buyers . . . what are their preferences vs male buyers

RESEARCH DESIGN

The following variables were hypothesized . . .
List of hypotheses

OPERATIONAL DEFINITIONS

List the specific variables and how you measured them

METHOD

Explain your sample . . . how you determined it . . . how you collected the data..
You can include a copy of the questionnaire here if used . . .

ANALYSIS OF RESULTS

Discuss how your hypotheses can out . . . Include "recommendations" here if appropriate . . .
OR: create a separate heading for recommendations

CONCLUSION

Some times this is inferred in your recommendations . . . Your conclusions will be credible if you address each of the above sections thoroughly

Printed in the United States
By Bookmasters

EPITAPH TO THE MATTRESS TAG!

Parents shouldn't tell kids stories like that. Even as a joke. The foot steps I heard and feet, of course, belonged to my dad. He had come to see if I was okay. He had forgotten about the mattress tag. It was 1944-45 and practice air raids were quite common. I was a little kid and believed my dad about the Mattress tag. When the sirens sounded in the still of the night and all of the lights went out, the vision of storm troopers coming to take me away and put me into a dark room with no lights was made all to real when I heard my dad's footsteps coming down the dark hallway in the dark of the night. All I could see from under the bed in the dim glow of the flashlight he was carrying, was a pair of feet thumping on the hardwood floor coming in my direction!

Scared the hell out me! You better believe it!

I have never touched a mattress tag since!

MAD ELEPHANT!

By Will Davis

I looked at that elephant's
Beady, little fiery, red eye
And knew he was angry at me.
I ran like hell and didn't stop,
Until I was as far away as I could be.
I do not know what I had done,
That had made him quite so angry.
When I had finished my fearful run,
And sat upon the hard wet ground,
Gasping and breathing rather heavily,
I heard a familiar sound in the distance.
And when I looked up, I could see
That angry elephant was still after me!
I could not run any further,
And waited for him to come to me.
He stopped in front of me,
With both those mad-looking,
Beady little red eyes and,
Stared directly at me.
Reached out unexpectedly,
With his snake-like nose,
And wrapped it around my waist.
I truly thought it was the end of me.
Raised me up and curled his trunk;
Rolled me up unceremoniously.
Like a pretzel, and he carried me
Back to the circus grounds.
He was as tender as he could be,
With his gentle handling of me.
Carried me to the full to the brim water barrel,
And dumped me in head first to the waist,
And swished me around repeatedly.
Then he gently placed me upon the ground,
And walked away with tail and trunk,
Swinging to and fro quite happily.

PESKY CRITTERS!

By Will Davis

The Statue of Liberty stands so tall!
The symbol of freedom for us all.
It's such a shame it had to be done.
The pest control people had to come.
The caretaker called the exterminator, you see.
Invaded by pesky critters was the Statue of Liberty!
They were into every nook and cranny.
The food they nibbled on quite happily,
As they ran amuck all over this island,
That the U. S. government named Liberty!
The statue stood tall and straight,
While within the pesky vermin ate.
They chewed upon anything they could get.
They even chewed on those disgusting cigarettes!
The exterminators did their job.
At day's end, the statue was entirely free of that mob.
But, the very next day, it did not work so well,
Because those peaky, testy, swarming vermin
Came back to invade the statue again!
There was not much that could be done,
Because after all, those pesky critters
Were just very curious humans!

Isn't it nice to know that in this country you can poke fun at such a grand old monument as the Statue of Liberty without fear of retribution from our government?

LITTLE FLY ON THE WALL!

By Will Davis

Little fly on the wall,
How come it is
That you don't fall?
What is your secret?
Please do tell us all.
We won't hurt you,
At this particular time.
We are curious, you see,
As we write this rhyme.
Tell us your secret,
Please do.
We want to walk,
The walls like you!
To be able to go anywhere
At any time,
When it pleases us to do;
To walk the walls like you.
Don't fly away just yet.
Your secret we have to get.
So we can go and have fun,
Buzzing around the town,
Until we find
A place to set down.
To be able to upset that clown
Who turns frowns upside down.
To buzz about his head,
As he swats at us!
Until he kills us dead!

this little ditty took me just ten minutes to think up and write. It has no particular meaning. just a fun thing to do to pass the time this evening. enjoy it if you will, for it was writen in fun with no intended pun.

THE BIG TOP!

By Will Davis

As I and the other kids watched
The lions, tigers, panthers, and bears,
As they dutifully performed their acts,
In wonderful wide open-eyed stares.
Eating cotton candy and popcorn,
Eyeing the clowns whenever they drew near,
Wondering what foolish trick they would do next.
As the peels of laughter roared about us with the cheers.
Applauding the high wire acts performed without fear,
As the scantily clad men and women danced about merrily,
On those invisible wires strung up so high.
As the adults watched once more through a child's eyes,
The wondrous awe, as the acrobats flew up to the sky.
Cheering and applauding so loudly.
As each routine was perfectly executed.
Marveled that they performed so effortlessly!
As many of us wished we could fly so expertly.
Down to earth we came when the acts were completely done.
More clowns and playful animals did we see.
As the trained animals performed their acts so expertly.
Then all too soon, the show was finally done!
And we went home completely happy and satisfied that we had come.
Me and my brother were asleep in the back seat of the car.

OH, TO BE A BOY AGAIN!

By Will Davis

What better way to celebrate life,
Than to climb a tree up to the sky!
To be carefree and not worry about strife!
To enjoy our youth and not wonder why.

To be as a young lad,
Free of all the worlds of pain.
To roam about the forests and plains;
To drink it all in like a child again!

Running and playing with your best friend.
Hearing his excited yelps and barks of joy.
Running and chasing after the rubber ball,
As he plays with his master; the young boy.

Or digging for creepy, crawling things!
Hunting for worms and all kinds of bugs,
To use as bait when you go fishing.
Sometimes running home for your mother's hugs.

Maybe to join in with your friends,
In the many varied games you love to play.
Searching and finding various uckee things
To chase the girls with, while the games you play.

Riding your bicycle all around town,
Just to see the familiar sights and to hear the sounds.
Feeling the thrill of it all with the wind in your face,
As you take in all that you've seen many times a thousand.

When at day's end, you go home,
Where love and warm food await your enjoyment,
And you do your share of the family chores.
When completed, you lie on the parlor floor.

Listening to your parents while you watch T. V.
Occasionally bothered by your brother or your sister.
Once in a while, playing with the cat,
That for some reason, you named 'Mister

Bed time finally arrives and off you go,
So you can be assured of a good nights sleep.
Perhaps to dream of days to come.
Building memories you shall forever keep!

ODE TO THE MOUSE
or wait until I get you—you little sucker!

By W.C. Davis

I was sitting in my parlor one day
Sipping a brew and reading the paper,
When out of the corner of my eye,
A moving shadow I did spy.

I paid it no never mind.
As when I went to investigate,
To my dismay and chagrin,
My chair I did vacate.

There was nothing to see;
Nothing there for me to see.
Nonplused, I took my seat again.
Took up my paper to read again.

Thought nothing of it,
'Til I saw the shadow once again
Flitting across the floor with great speed,
Faster than the fittest of steeds.

There was naught for me to do,
But purchase a trap or two.
Setting them out strategically,
In hopes of getting one or two.

The first trap was a success.
One was trapped and removed.
Two days later, another succumbed.
Then to my great surprise,

There was a great big giant one!
Black with a big, fat, white belly!
I did not get to see his eyes,
For he was too quick for me to see!

As he scampered to and fro
Enjoying his newfound freedom,
I was perplexed that he remained free
For the traps he did avoid.

No matter the place or type of food,
He circled them with great ease.
Ran right over them as though they weren't there
And right across the top of my chair.

More traps I laid out for him.
To him, the fun was about to begin.
With great care and dexterity
He ate the cheese quite delicately.

Then scampered away in glee.
I could have sworn he was laughing at me!
More traps just wouldn't do.
There were enough, don't you see.

It would be just a matter of time
Before he would finally spend his time
Caught in one of those devices.
Squealing to be set free!

The next day at rest I was,
In my favorite easy chair.
Next to the bookcase you see,
When I reached out for a book to read.

Just as my hand touched the spine of the book,
Some instinct, at the bookcase, made me look.
There it sat, staring at me in all its proud little glory,
With what appeared to be a big wide grin, you see!

Just you wait and see! Ha! Ha! Ha!
Just you wait and see! Ha! Ha! Ha!
That dirty little fiend! That devil's apparition
Won't get the best of me! Ha! Ha! Ha!

I'm not quite sure, you see,
But I think he is getting the best of me!
I am not ready to give in.
I've just begun to fight, you see!

I cannot and will not let that
Little beast get the best of me.
I'm bigger than he is, and much smarter, too.
I am bound to see that creature caged in a zoo!

But when he sits and laughs at me,
That's more than I can stand to bear.
So the next time he shows, I must prepare,
To set the best of traps that there be.

I hope that when this is all done,
That he will be the only one.
Chasing mice is not my thing.
I'd rather be out dancing and dining.

It is not that I am being mean,
But that—and—little thing
Just doesn't belong in my abode.
So in the only way I know, he must be told!

He does not belong in this household!
A pet he shall not become.
His qualifications are not the best.
I'm searching for words to put this tale to rest.

A magic wand I could most assuredly use.
I know that I would put it to very good use.
I know my tale is quite not told.
For the mouse is much too much bold!

He still runs about free, you see.
Laughing at me, don't you see?
But his days are numbered for sure,
Because I'm about to shut his door!

This you must assuredly know,
There are no barriers for a mouse.
No matter the precautions,
He will find a way into your house!

In our most famous historic past,
The greatest of tales of mice abound.
The mouse has proven to be
The most durable mammal found!

From the fantastic Christmas stories
From yesterday and to those beyond.
There is no other more unwelcomed beast
To <u>not</u> be invited to the great family holiday feast!

Intelligent though it may well be,
This four-legged, creepy little creature,
Will become, as you all most definitely will see,
The big stupendous, and glorious main feature!

When upon that celebrated day,
He will become as no more.
When into my trap, he will stray,
To be as Poe's famous "NEVERMORE!"

I have planned extremely well.
With all of his smarts, he has learned
Of the many traps in his path, I have placed.
So I move them about with great care and concern.

In hopes that he will soon be captured.
Then all of my mouse problems
Will then be put to their final rest.
My home will then be rid of this pest!

As I retire upon Christmas Eve,
To dream of peace and the gifts,
I most definitely will happily receive.
A rustling and movement in the shadows is perceived!

I have come to a great realization,
That I am, quite honestly, to be a victim,
To that mouse's happy celebration,
Of that famous night in question.

Why did that creature have to pick on me!?
I was as happy in my home as I could be.
I know for sure, that Santa did not give him to me.
Where he came from is a great mystery.

I am hoping and praying to the powers that be,
That this small creature's visit to me,
Will be the end of it's short comings,
And the beginning of it's long goings for me.

The cheese I place upon the trap so delicately.
So my fingers do not get snapped so heavily.
He removes so carefully and stealthily.
To my great dismay to find the trap undisturbed and empty!

He has learned from my administrations,
To capture him with no quarter given,
To remove him from my presence,
He has proven to be very sneaky and unforgiving.

My tale has come to an unresolved end.
I will continue to stalk and trail him.
To ply him with all of the goodies that I can,
Until he is captured and put away for good!

You know, don't you, that this is not really the end.
That this mouse just, quite possibly, might win in the end.
And follow me to the grave, when at life's end,
To our respective resting places we shall end.

I know that I will eventually have to go,
When to my grave I will descend.
Know this for sure, and with great certainty,
That little beast will most assuredly go before me!

THE CIRCUS!
(Through the eyes of a ten-year-old boy)

By Will Davis

I went to the circus the other day.
I got to see all of the clowns do their thing.
But most of all—the most important thing
Was I got to see all of the animals at play!
I got to eat popcorn, peanuts, and cotton candy,
Hamburgers, hot dogs, and many other things!
But the strangest of all was I got to eat
These great big elephant ears!
The money I spent filled my daddy's eyes with tears!
Before we went home and called it a day.
When all of the shows were completed and done,
We got to visit all of the animals, one by one.
The biggest of all were those huge, gray, behemoths!
With short, rope-like tails and their long serpentine noses,
They were great things of wonder to see.
I paid no mind to the warnings issued to me.
I was under the wrong end you see!
And that great big behemoth of an elephant,
Quite unceremoniously proceeded to poop all over me!

Based upon a true event!

HOT DOGS!

By Will Davis

I was preparing hot dogs
For a meal the other day.
When a very young friend
Happened to come my way.

He watched with great interest,
As my meal I prepared to eat.
I put the dogs in some buns,
And he said how that looked so neat.

I began to apply the condiments.
Then into the bun, that dog went.
When I applied the yellow mustard,
He said, "That looks just like my puppy's POOP!"

When he had gone on his way,
I looked at that hot dog in a bun,
And came to the realization,
That, that little boy had spoiled my fun in a bun!

Composed 8-26-2008 at 2:00 p.m., while cooking hot dogs for a snack!

ABOUT THE AUTHOR

This is my first attempt at getting published nationally. From my days in high school, and as far back as I can remember in grade school, I liked to write. I began writing my poetry to impress a girl younger than I of my romantic intentions. Bear in mind, I was a high school kid at that time. I continued to write many more poems about all subjects down through the years. Unfortunately, during my hitch in the Air Force, more than two hundred poems that I had written and kept in the bottom of my bedroom closet were lost! My dad, in the process of spring cleaning, had found my box of poetry written upon many scraps of paper. He didn't think they were of any value and tossed them into the garbage, along with my comic book collection (which I think he gave to a relative). Fortunately, at least fifty to sixty were saved, and I continued to add to them over the years in my spare time. To date, I have written close to 200 poems, which I hope to have published. Enclosed is a selection of poems written with kids in mind. Many of these were written after I retired, and were based upon true events or ideas I had gotten from out of nowhere. The one titled, "HOT DOG!" and "THE LITTLE MOUSE!" was written just a few weeks ago.

Here, then, are my poetic endeavors, which I hope will be received enthusiastically.

Printed in the United States
By Bookmasters